NASHVILLE - LOS ANGELES - NEW YORK

WRITEBLOODY
QUALITY AMERICAN BOOKS AND PRINTING

UNCONTROLLED EXPERIMENTS IN FREEDOM

RILEY'S
RED WAGON BOOK SWAP
THE TOLEDO @ CORONA
LONG BEACH

BY: BRIAN STEPHEN ELLIS

You have made me consider tatooing my chest.

[signature]

WRITE BLOODY PUBLISING 2008

Uncontrolled Experiments in Freedom is a book of poetry documenting the manic and shimmering life of Brian Stephen Ellis. His narratives come from the images of a world where many believe no poetry to exist. This is a second-hand microscope examining the fuzzy science of survival. Enjoy.

THANK YOU

Simone Beaubien, Adam Foam, Francis
Joseph Deignan, Shira Erlichman, Justin
Taylor, Kate Lee, Casey Rocheteau, Brian
Lawlor, Morgan Shaker, Shane Donnelly,
Gregory James Mullen, Greta Merrick,
Brandon Plumert, James Caroline, Brian
Purtle, Chris Redgate, Adam Stone,
Ryler Dustin, Judy, Buddy Wakefield, The
Whitehaus Family, The Cantab Family,
Bruce, Peter, Mom, Dad

TABLE OF CONTENTS

UNCONTROLLED EXPERIMENTS IN FREEDOM

"RELAX...THIS WON'T HURT"

- Hunter S. Thompson

Hunter S. Thompson exit note illustration
by shea M gauer

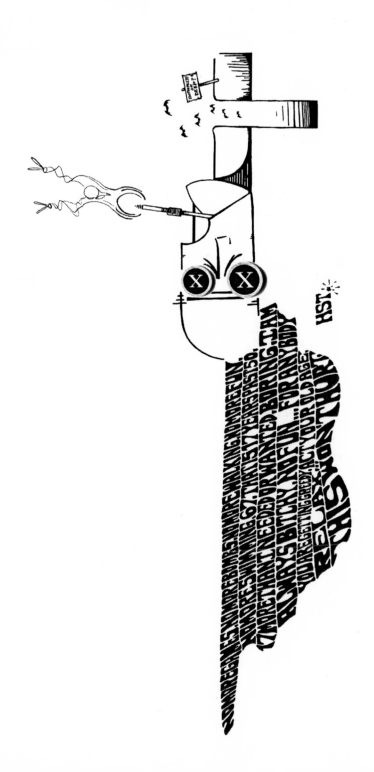

SHOPPING CARTS

It started as a game of Communist Soccer
Communist Soccer is when you and your friends
stand around a shopping cart, volleying the ball back and forth
eventually getting it in the basket

In Communist Soccer, when one person gets it in the basket
everyone does

We had the energy, we had the night, we had each other
We had a problem,
we were way too good at this
So we did the most obvious thing: we stacked another
shopping cart on top of the one we already had
But a hot minute later we were popping the ball in
every other slap of the ankle

By the time we lifted that third cart in the air
we knew something unexpected was going on…
maybe even something magical

The Shopping Carts, they were begging for it
Begging for us to pull pyramids out of them
So we answered their prayers
The logistics were immediate
and the mechanics came even quicker

We worked in pairs, gathering the carts, lifting and attaching,
deciding where the sculpture was going to go next
First the center is upright and then
we spread outward,
laying the carts on their sides
The next layer rests with its front wheels
hooked into the basket in the center

You wouldn't suspect how many ways
shopping carts can lock into one another
In the middle of an empty Stop & Shop parking lot on a weeknight
It didn't take long for authority to come after us
And we ran, but not before we we're given a thick:

"Hey! you think this is funny? Who's gonna take this down?"

Some lifetime-dead-end-job schlub just like me
whose morning routine will be abruptly interrupted by something
he/she didn't know existed

Our work was not finished

At Star Market we erected an overflowing swarm
of metal and carriage

By the dumpsters of Family Dollar we recollected the scattered bones
of commercialism into a throne of modern antiquity
We slid them upside-down into the ones right-side up
We forced wheels into handles

In the alley behind Toys 'r' Us we erected a ziggurat
to the possibilities of shopping carts

It was what was inside of us
and like everything else
it came from the earth

We chiseled away all that was not shopping cart from the air
and the closer we drew
to the realm of the impossible, the larger it became

We wrote letters, in the language of shopping cart,
and they read:

Wage Slave,
When you pull this apart tomorrow, please,
do not let any weight gather in your shoulders
We wanted to put a little impossible in your life again
a little unexpected, a little
'I-don't-know-what's-around-the-corner'
and we wanted to remind you of the necessity of magic
So when you pull apart these structures, sculptures, pyramids
remember that a pyramid has five points
One
that aims toward god
and four
that aim for something more important

ELEVEN TO SEVEN

I arrive at 10:30 and the high-schoolers
arrive fifteen minutes later
on their way home
from the liquor store, getting mixers

At 11 my shift starts and it all
begins a half-an-hour later
When the evening shift nurses get off duty
they buy their low-tar cigarettes and clear out

Next the nightclub crowd washes in
for a pit stop before they hit main street

The single mothers that live in the neighborhood
behind the convenience store file in after that
filing in with those hapless, loveable stoners
who are always looking for that same thing
that they never find

12:30 and the waitresses drag themselves in
They and I share the same meager smile

By one, those nightclubbers have got
their drunk on, and are crashing their way back home,
buying condoms and the pack of cigarettes
they thought that they didn't need

At 1:30 the newspaper delivery drivers purchase
over-the-counter amphetamines
and fill up their station wagons

Two o'clock belongs to the cab drivers
howling and yelping and blowing off steam
from twelve hours of bad tips

At 2:30 I fall asleep

When convenience stores sleep,
they dream that they're hospitals

or, at the very least, the cursed king of sustenance
whose touch turns everything to cancer
From the slave trade coffee
to the world war gasoline, let's face it
everything in here is poison

So when the trailer truck driver shows up at three a.m.
the only thing I have to offer this man is me
He buys a pack of Camel Lights outta politeness
and hangs out by the register, telling me
about a lousy route, on a lousy road
in a lousy land that never gets more forgiving
His eyes are begging me not to become him
His heart is dying not to be my martyr

The other four nights of the week
3 a.m. is all stillness and frailty

But on Friday nights 3 a.m. is a man
whose skin is burnt by the nickelodeon of yellow lines
Whose knees ache from the hum of a gas pedal
Who gets paid just to stay awake
Who gets paid to never stop moving
Someone like me,
whose shoulders burn from constantly shoving
the stupid, stupid night
into morning

Four a.m. brings the airport employees to work

Five a.m. is an assistant manager who doubts my intelligence

By six a.m. I'm dead

And by seven, I'm driving home
My retinas scoured by the details
of all the tiny, unrecorded movements
of humans

FINGERTIP GUNFIRE

Christopher Redgate collects photographs
of people he doesn't know

My mother collects ceramic figurines of owls

I collect dead-end jobs

This is a difficult hobby to maintain
The larger my collection grows
the greater the suspicion of my new employers
I used to construct intricate fables in
the 'previous experience' boxes on my applications
No more
Now, I only write one sentence on my job applications:

Motherfucker, I Speak Register as a Second Language

I don't care how angry your customers are
I don't care how long the line is
I don't care how many items you got
I will cradle your purchases in my hands
like refugees and in their own memories
I will ring the sale with the precision of a sextant

My fingers are changeling, my fingers are liquid
My fingers are a cloud of exploding diamond gas
My fingers are lawn mowers with laser fan blades

The index and middle punch in the dollars
and the ring jams on the decimal
then it's back to the middle to enter the coins, if any
I roll my pinky over the total, and,
PFFHTFP-KRHRSSHH...

the fender dinosaur squeal of quarters,
the frantic jazz high hat of dimes,
the hollow baritone of nickels,
the ancient marching band of pennies,

My hands are translators of copper and paper dialects
They know nothing of numbers, and everything of dancing
My hands have seen ten years of clinging to the bottom rung
My hands probably should've learned more in the past decade
than how to smile in the face of lazy american disrespect

Go ahead, check your receipt
I don't make mistakes
I don't want to talk about the price of your lifestyle
If you think something costs too much
Don't Buy It,
you probably don't need it anyway

Here's an idea: put me out of a job
I was looking to expand my collection anyway
Better yet, put the slave that made that item out of a job
I dare you

But don't even consider interrupting how gorgeous
my movements are
This is the only foreign language I know
This is the only musical instrument I can play

You may have all the time in the world
but I'm doubling in age every day
and I don't have enough time left in my life
to be as beautiful as I want to be

So I want you to know:
I can't let you get in the way
of my music

MEXICAN TRANQUILIZER LOVESONG

You are nineteen, young, and innocent enough
You can't yet grow hair on your face
You've never lived outside your parents' home
You haven't yet memorized the cold echo of ketamine
as it vacuums into your sinuses
like the hissing sound the sun makes
as it guillotines into six o'clock

You are nineteen, and romantic
and you and your eleven best friends move into
a three-bedroom home
A family of dropouts and shut-ins,
of criminals, and ravers, and life-experimenters

The first thing you do is throw out all of your clocks
You replace them with high-schoolers
who show up every day in time to miss first period,
bringing the morning and hangovers in their back pockets
This is where the party ended each night
There were mornings hiding around every corner
So you kept the shades drawn all day long
but drawn shades are a lousy substitute for sunset.

Your telephone lines withered and died
The television was shut off a week ago
You stop working so you have enough time
to make money, going on long journeys
made of many short deliveries,
You are nineteen
and for the first time
your life has a purpose
For the first time, you're an over-achiever

Sometimes, if you were lucky,
the weekend enveloped you like a mushroom cloud
and you and your family hunkered down and locked in,
getting lost in the maze you built together,
fashioned out of blacklights and police-beckoning techno,
filling your ears with anonymous electric heartbeats,
hammered into the rhythm of windshield-wiper blades
and c-c-cut over late nineties Madonna

"Don't tell me to stop"
Rhythm was a direction and each drug a new religion,
pounding like the hearts of racehorses for your faith
The odds-on favorite: Ketamine,
whose smell was the north star as it cooked
on the double boiler
turning from liquid to salt

Later in life, when people ask you how you so casually
started doing drugs,
you won't know what to say

You'll mutter something about how sometimes
arrogance is a prayer
You'll say something about how you can get trapped
by the exhilaration you feel
from the safety of doing dangerous things in groups
But you won't talk
about the love of a family born of a moment
Born of a night, that went on for months
a love that you earned for the first time, you earned

Because the best part of being indestructible
is forgetting that you are
And the best part of doing drugs
is being alive afterwards
The best part is flinging yourself
further than anyone can reach
and still landing safely in someone's arms

There were mornings hiding around every corner
and one morning, the sun found you
and we weren't a family any more
That was all that had saved us

VOMITING IN THE MEN'S ROOM AT BICKFORD'S, IN HANOVER, MASSACHUSETTS

I made it out of the backseat of the car,
I made the 999 steps to the door,
I made it past the morning crowd,
the waitress, the ordering...
But halfway through my tall stack
of strawberry sugar, butter and blueberry syrup...
I lost it.

Eighteen seconds ago I was drunk.
Now I'm hunched over the toilet in the men's bathroom
 at Bickford's, in Hanover, MA.
My stomach unfolds into my throat
and my mouth blossoms into a sunset bouquet
blossoms into a sunset bouquet of fruit, starch and bile

At this moment, I am perfect.
In this instant my body contains no awareness of self
I am only the act of vomiting
This is the kind of zen
middle-aged pseudo-bohemian assholes
have wet dreams about

As I fall back onto the thousands of tiny tiles
that make up the bathroom floor,
nothing exists
Outside the guzzling ocean-tongued vacuum
pogo-sticking on my temples

I will puke three times in the eighteen
breathless minutes I spend here
a lifetime married to these tiles,
and the porcelain, and the urine-soaked bolts that
hold this toilet to the bottom of the world
We will build a house together
inside a bead of sweat on my forehead,
which is really a fever tear
shed by my skeleton, gasping for air,

while a lightning rod of a yawning alarm clock
shudders between my eyebrows and eyelashes
From the door of that house
I will cajole my humanity back
while it sloshes around me
in a see-sawing orbit,
memorizing pinpricks of the toilet stall:
-ancient scraps of torn toilet paper trapped in the dispenser
-the pattern of the flickering lights
-Janis luvs 2 git gangbanged (508)-3xx-x7x5

The problem is,
bathroom stall doors don't go all the way down to the floor
Any minute now some dusty early bird will discover me,
a manic heap of the night before
So as I leave that house I make myself a promise:
Not to forget all that has transpired here
And in three hundred and thirty three seconds

I break that promise.

WET

After we all moved in, Julian talked to us less and less
tip-toed down the kool-aid/smirnoff stained
hallway, when he came out of his room
bought a lock for his door
After eating three or four pills of ectascy
for three or four days your body
doesn't have the serotonin to give you
much entertainment
Julian is a cutter

He came out to get the kitchen knife with
an anime sort of flourish
I don't know if I was the only one who noticed
and I didn't know what I was doing
the flimsy wood of the suburban door rattled
in the frame when it struck my extended right foot
tick-tocking in its hinges
my older brother's voice came out of my mouth
Julian didn't want to hear it
Just by stepping in, I was going too far
I didn't know what I was talking about
but I was talking
I grabbed the knife handle, we fell to the bed

He told me I was stupid
He wanted it for sentimental reasons
He said that if he wanted to kill himself then he
could just shatter his full length mirror
I tried not to think about how
breaking glass sounds wet

the orgy of our fists rocked a drunken
rowboat dance in the sharp glow
from across the hall
the cheap infomercial blade cast
patches of light around our adolescence
like washed out silhouettes of moths jerking
and dipping in lazy haloes
Julian was stronger than me but I wouldn't shut up

the knife swung into my palm

skin popping like the balloon of salt that it is
the glare turned saffron

Julian gasped, we both let go of the handle
I bled on him a little

I stood up, my sneakers crunching on
the sand on the hardwood floors
where we lived then it was impossible to escape
the sand, the father of glass

ANONYMOOSE PUNK RAWK (TO EAT, RUN, AND SLEEP BY)

Oh,
we were fucking running motherfucker!
and we ran fast!
because running was our occupation
but we weren't running from anything
we were stoned, and drunk
and had each taken a handful of amphetamines
and we were standing in Cumberland Farms, wondering
how the hell you sell 64 ounces of Slushie for 89 cents
and we assumed that Cumberland Farms clearly
owes a debt to the god of Slushies, but then again
Brian, Tim, Shauneene and I were never
any good at math, so we drove
and because we were driving,
we were drinking and you may say that
that doesn't make any sense,
and you're right it doesn't
because you shouldn't be able to tip a jug of Carlo Rossi
all the way upside-down in the backseat of a 94 Ford Taurus,
but somehow we managed

Tim knew a really great rock wall to climb
so we drove for 63 minutes in a straight line
and by the time we had snuck through two
backyards and a fence that said 'No Trespassing'
it wasn't trespassing, it was responsibility
we stayed at the top of that rock wall long enough
to smoke a cigarette
then we drove in the opposite direction for twice
as long, blaring 63 different two-minute songs
hoping that if we drove fast enough
the songs would never catch up with us

We dropped in on an old friend
who used to be called Craphog,
but no longer deserved the honor of the title
and by the time we had broken in and
woke up his girlfriend, we all understood
that this was a tribute and a punishment at once

we played the Marvel Super Heroes trivia game
at just after 3:33 in the morning, and I won
because I knew Charles Francis Xavier's middle name
we left Craphog behind
and drove to the beach
to watch the sun come up
it didn't
instead it rained
and we wondered if finally, for once,
the sun got to the horizon and said
". . . fuck it"

we went back to the car
and didn't matter where we went
or how we got there
or that we even went anywhere at all
because even when we were standing still
we were doing it as quickly as possible

JOHNNY OZONE

They call him Johnny Ozone
because while his buddies were popping pills
he was popping the tops off
of Dust-off and Air Freshener
Backfiring his brain into comfortable paralysis,
Laying in the bushes behind trailer parks and locked
in the bathrooms of motels that you can see from the highway,
but only the locals know how to get to them

Johnny Ozone is the story that lives in everyone's closet;
never bothered nobody,
just wanted to know if he could crash on your couch
or under your sink
Doesn't talk or eat much
Pasty skin dangling from skeletal frame
Called him zombie behind his back

His ex-girlfriend was at work when it happened
He was sitting on her bed,
Johnny Ozone took a single ever-widening breath,
His tongue made a noise like a vacuum,
His eyes rolled back,
But instead of hitting the wall,
they kept on rolling
His brain boiled over
and his heart stopped

That's where I found him

Now, ghosts can't cross running water.
That's why our hearts beat
How else would your spirit stay inside of you?

When Johnny Ozone's heart stopped
there was no longer anything to keep ME out
I entered through his nostrils,
wading through the bloody swamp of his sinuses,
and climbed into his brain

In the antiseptic fog I found that all of his wit and intelligence
was still there, frozen in chemical rust
I discovered the kindling of ten years of creativity unused
I found all of his favorite memories: the skateboards,
the breasts, the Zeppelin albums... and like puzzle pieces
I fit them back into their fluorocarbon holes

I burrowed down into his ribcage and
when I had scrubbed away all the sludge,
I found a heart that had grown so small
it no longer had any room for fear

Because death will come and go, but we are souls
and the only thing that binds us is running water
and the only place we have to hide is our bodies

And eighteen seconds after Johnny Ozone's heart stopped,
it started again
And I've been in here ever since

16

INDIANA OUTSIDE

I must have been turning
in my sleeping bag,
in the back of the station wagon
Floating on worn steel and minerals

1992 Buick Century
I knew we were moving before my eyelids turned on
My skin had memorized the vibration of the highway
Everything came back to me piece by piece

On the last day of work as night manager of Family Dollar,
I locked up the place and left with three trash bags
full of everything we thought would be useful

We drove a night and a day and a night
and when I lifted my humming forehead
from under the sleeping bag
Katie said, "Boo, look at this..."

It was Indiana outside, and the land
lifted like it knew us
The horizon shimmered above the borderland
of second-grade landscapes, where children,
in their infinite wisdom, leave the universe blank

Each second I was further than I had ever been
from Manchester, New Hampshire
and the earth erupted out of the sun
and it was morning in another land

People had questions about mine and Katie's relationship
But I never loved Katie as
much as the things she did...

Her ability to move without question
Her ability to drive in the night
I didn't love her as much as the fact that I felt safe with her
My older brother thought I was helping her run away

Descendants of the coast are often endowed
with a seventh sense:
They can always tell how far they are from the ocean
Getting too far inland, they become afraid

In Indiana
the earth never separates from the sun
and the night is not dark but burnt
in the shadow of clashing flames

We couldn't have been running away
because runaways are people who move further and further
and further from home,
and we were most certainly going towards it

Runaways are out to forget, and we
were trying to memorize

Runaways are motion, even when
standing still
But Katie and I, we never stopped moving
and home was always on the other side
of the eruption of earth

It is a good thing that there's no ocean
in Indiana, because the sailors and the runaways
would have most certainly gotten lost
when the sun rose in every direction

MOUNTING THE EARTH

Escalator stairs are born in the gear-filled center of the earth
Escalator stair nurseries are cold,
dark places that stink of mercury and ash
Their infancy, their entire childhood,
is tremendously brief
The Great Gear Gargollisk
will click its tongue only nine times
before an escalator stair becomes an adult

Escalator stair society is brutal
Education and training are closely overseen
Failure is not accepted. Even their only recreation,
The Dance,
is preparation in disguise

Every aspect of the escalator stair's life is streamlined
Every escalator stair has both sex organs
and gender is simply the direction you face
An escalator stair's training is only finished
when the Great Escallidine says so

It takes an escalator stair
one hundred years
to travel to the surface of the earth
This is the Great Pilgrimage
At its end is The Great Crossing Over

The moments when an escalator stair emerges
will be the only time it comes out from under the earth

These few moments will justify a lifetime of preparation

These few moments will decide an escalator stair's worth

It is the only time the escalator stair will feel
any kind of purpose. Here, thousands of miles
from the heart of the earth where the stair was born,
will be the only place it will know as home

When these moments pass,
the escalator stair will be swallowed
by those hideous metal teeth
and never seen again

May We All Be So Lucky

95

Six months
unraveled like a busted cassette tape and
wrapped around my fingers
fingers wrapped around a steering wheel

this convenience store clerk became a cab driver
they named me 95

forty five hours a week divided into three fifteen-hour shifts
that we called Friday, Saturday, and Sunday
for the night shift you work two–to-two,
or two-to-five if you were desperate
I was desperate

they told me my name was 95
and **to go where I just fucking…
are you listening, jackass?**…they said
but what their flat faces, that had lost
the ability to smile or frown, really said was
*welcome to our slot machine and, despite everything,
this is honorable work, this is our living*

Friday started with the sound of an entire county
cashing their paychecks
Friday came to mean trailer park shopping sprees,
sprees as regular as section 8 reviews
Friday night tips better because It thinks that this weekend
is going to be different

you make friends
this stop light, that stop light, parking lot, parking lot
the stop signs seem to glow on their own
when things were working I could lock into
a pattern of lights and direction and taking calls
the more bodies that climb into the back
the more bodies I move
the more I made
the money that kept me fed
the money that kept me in a home

Saturday afternoon can't hide what it's preparing for
it doesn't even try
Saturday night is collapsing after itself
frozen in the act of forgetting that it will end

I slap-dash in slutty orbits, around bright bars and shimmering
homes

One a.m. Saturday night Main Street Hyannis is the relay race
that sociology forgot
brake lights and open signs seesaw on and off
amongst the throngs of lonely drunks
waiting for the ocean to change to their color

buildings are dark sharp shapes dancing between the vaporous
fingernails of The Glowing

faces are the same.

22

the end of each shift is an experiment in rediscovering morning
the night is infinite
but only as long as it lasts
like a dream

the summer night's worn pale from too much friction, partying,
driving
as I slide from exit seven back to the center of Hyannis
and drive under the landing lights of the airport,
obese, low-hanging stars, churning a candescent weathered dandelion
flat against the off-grey clouds
lightning-thin and eager to melt into the afternoon
on the other side of forever

the earth so still
that it must be the sun that revolves
around our murmuring lives

Hyannis has a low ceiling
I can feel it hanging limp-waisted
on my deadening eyes

I wake up
and I'm in the cab and the dispatcher is screaming,

**95! this is why we don't hire twenty-motherfucking-
year-old cab drivers! are you there? 95!**

Sunday is as stupid as things that wake up
Sunday needs a ride home from the hospital
because Saturday didn't know how to stop
Sunday night is a desperate prostitute
offering me stolen jewelry
to give her a ride to the homeless shelter

I am passed from neighborhood to neighborhood
until I put all the strangers where they belong
the strangers slide into my metal body
and I am surprised every time they
turn out to be a person
but I keep moving and the strangers become something else
All Of The Traffic Lights in Hyannis
Are Waiting For My Eyes To Change Color

Are you there yet? 95?

Six months
unraveled like a busted cassette tape and wrapped around
a place that's become like a person to me
I am moving
my body is moving
and I am living

Are you there?

if time was space then events would be places
and verbs would be nouns
I am moving
I am living

Are you there?

human beings feel the most alive
when we are more than ourselves
when our actions
are like locations

Are you there yet? 95?

NO THRU WAY

When I came out of the bathroom
I must've had some coke on my nose because Hobbes
gave me the signal: (upperlipbrushbrushbrush)

He was in the hallway talking to Melody,
fifteen and hefting an unbreakable handle of vodka
that was twice her weight,
Draped in stolen manufacturer-torn black clothes,
her eyes bruised from the internet and middle age,

Stumbling out of bathrooms and learning to hold it in
in the one-floor houses that hang to the outer rims
of byzantine cul-de-sacs that you can only navigate into,

She tells him, "I'm going to be president one day."
and when she says this,
I hope everything I've ever learned about
the world is wrong

The hairs on my forearms have just turned to helium
The roof of my mouth tastes like the bottom of a burnt Pyrex plate
I am moving faster than I realize down an unfinished staircase
to a basement bedroom cramped with the population of our heritage
and I step into the moment that this night began

After the bar, after Tiki Port, driving the '94 Ford Taurus
punchy, sharp and tumbling,
like climbing down pine trees head-first,
like a cocaine binge,
to this wedge of a place with a dirt driveway and broken '80s sports cars
tucked around the side of the house, sinking into the crabgrass
like the skeletons of dogs that kill

The screen to this aluminum outer door has been missing
since the year my car was made
This house that rose out of the dirt,
not much more than a fistful of unwanted generations
This living room like a hole in the neck,
the vacuum of lineage

And the big screen, the Playstation One, the pile of unpaid cable bills,
the soiled mottled couches, the sandy threadbare carpets,
there's a sink full of drinking problems
and you're in the kitchen taking shots
with somebody's mom
while the kids crash dirty hurricane around you

These expectations haven't been lowered
so much as ground down,
into the sand crunching under
tattered sweatshop sneakers,
whispering for you to
give up
like winter in a tourist town

Illio has got a bunch of meth on him, but he's holding back,
enjoying the attention, knowing that as soon as he busts it out
everyone will want to get in on it
and soon, there's another decade gone

In the opposite corner is Karrenna
a pregnant twenty-four-year-old mother of two
who holds up a ziplock bag of cocaine
and asks if someone could, please
snort this so that she doesn't

Hobbes is upstairs,
playing with the kids
and wondering about evolution

He's thinking about the humanity we lost
searching for morals in the clicking tongues of razor-blades

How numb you get from the sand
and so we grow sharp like the barks of seagulls
He hopes the kids don't grow too tall,
that their muscles never become a shell,
that they don't get crushed like cardboard VHS sleeves,
that they don't twist their ankles running from the mystery sins
of fathers they've never met,
that their prayers don't drown in the howling of empty bottles,
kissed by the relentless Atlantic wind

Hobbes is thinking about the moment this night began
He's thinking about bottles,
spilled and spreading,
tucked under soiled mottled couches
in homes that were never made to look like nuclear physics

Cape Cod doesn't have any sewers,
we just put our shit in the ground
This is what we have grown out of

EMPTY PARKING LOTS

The good part
about living in your car
is that you wake up
and you're ready for the day
With no pretext of a bed to slow you down
With no shackles of comfort to hold you to sleep
It can be so easy to get up and start moving
Everything you control is in front of you;
the warped question mark of the steering wheel,
taking up your lap like an insistent housecat,
the thin mouth of the accelerator
hungry for feet
We're all hungry.

Hunger walks nervously along the long miles
of my intestines, incessantly shaking its rat-nest hair,
icicles flinging from out of the tangle

I imagine there is frozen bubble gum inside of my bones
and no amount of bookstore shuffling
or bank-lobby coffee will melt it

My joints sound like December pumpkins
bursting under fists of mischief

My face is Halloween misplaced

The bad mornings begin with the sarcastic tapping of police officers
I can see them, with their eyes,
trying to render me someone from another country,
someone who speaks broken something
I am a dirty sock in someone else's house
And these people, with houses,
who pretend that they deserve things
like bathrooms and orgasms

Now I understand why wars are fought.
What else is there besides
land and belonging?

Lacking the humanity of an address
but shaking the animal hood of the sick and the caged,
I am seen by your citizens as something in-between.

Once, they called us trolls.

This is where we live and where we die,
this is where we live, under bridges and behind trailer parks,
in mausoleum dumpsters and empty parking lots
This is where we live,
sucking the torn fingernails of death
into our goblin lungs
This is the curse of the broken,
to bear the shame of kings
to ceaselessly wander the labyrinth
of America's minotaur heart.

THE SWEAT ON THE PILLOW

The sprout becomes a tree

The tree grows West,
towards the sunset

Nearby, the river flows in three-second intervals,
licking the shore with white

Above, the sun's beams dice the earth
into perfect parallel lines
and the corn grows

The corn brings the locust
The sun makes the locust's muscles grow large

While fucking me in the ass
the locust nibbles at the base of my skull

until only the nightmares are left

My left testicle swells and falls off
It cracks open, and a baby tumbles out

The baby yawns and becomes a woman
with flowing blonde hair

She eats off my flesh, turning me to meat with itching

I join a circus of skeletons
The ringmaster beckons.

He splits open my skull
and covers my brain with melted sugar
and lowers me into a vat of ants

Everyone cheers

When the ants have finished with my eyes

I jolt awake

I'm in the cave, and I know that the bees
will be here any second

Suddenly there is a girl wearing a crown of water

She tells me, "The world was sung into existence

For each person who forgets his song, a dream

becomes a nightmare

To keep the bees away

you must start singing

and never stop."

ARGUING IN THE POST OFFICE

There's that exhausting, but sexy feeling
knowing that you're the one who's going
to fuck up the line at the post office

You can almost read lines of dialogue
scrolling backwards on our irises,
"I am going to make you late for work"

The font on post office forms has
an innocent mathematical voice,
like a baby robot
I do my best to fill in simple answers
the clerk hands it back after a quick glance
"Its not filled out."
I leave the paper in his hands,
"I wrote in all I could"

His face is a badge of worry
wrapped in detour signs
He has a sloppy crew cut
and the soft eyes of an elderly dog

At home, he has a box set
of John Wayne VHS sitting on a dusty mantle
next to a box set of Red Skelton
He spends a lot of time watching
really boring porn

"There's no address" He tastes each word
before spitting them out
Behind me, people are checking
and double-checking the passage of time

"Where do you get your mail?" He asks
"I don't. That why I'm applying for a PO Box."
His eyes are the white cracks
in the ice cubes of warm soda
His eyes are broken hockey blades

"Where do you live?"

"I, I don't have a place to live."

"We need to mail you this form to verify
that you have an address, then you bring
the form back in…we can't give you
a PO Box otherwise…people attempt
mail fraud all the time."

"That's okay," I tell him,

"I can live without it."

EVAPORATE

The rain got in
through the concrete, through the steel door
through the locks and the keys
It wouldn't stop

The rain fell in our bedroom all day and night
We were drenched

There were miles of fog between the door and the bed
but we always found our way

We awoke each morning knee-deep in the puddles
and each night the waters got deeper

Soon, they weren't puddles,
they were filling up the room
The water wrapping around the legs of the desk
curling into the closet, climbing into
and out of the dresser drawers,
soaking all of our clothes

The water lifted the bed off the floor
and now we were lost, on the island of it

Stranded all over each other

The rain could never be heard over the moans
which were deafened by the thunder
which was really your shoulders
which you pulverized me with
I've got broken noses all over my body

Eventually the rain submerged us
and we were drowning divers
Swimming skyward, our blood becoming dervishes
telling us to slow down
which of course we never could
as we locked on to one another for breath

And now I understand,
You and I are the same race after all
Our people were born to have their skin
seen in the lightning light

I guess, maybe, you're not supposed to have sex
in a thunderstorm
But what if it never rains again?

I feel sorry for every raindrop
that never gets to meet the skin
it was born to touch when
It evaporates as the lightning falls upon it
in its shot-put from heaven to the ocean

34

THE JANITOR POEM

the blood-shot eye of morning
buoys itself into lavender pre-dawn
like the second syllable for every word for the week

I am washing windows in my janitor's uniform
dirty with the stains of bleach and ammonia
that reek of the opposite of life

my water-burned fingertips sling sponge & rag & squeegee
over the cool six a.m. glass
licking the handprints and the sweat smog
from the entrance of the Mall

I will lope in a slow march
across the earth-tone tiles of this misguided colosseum
until nine when it's time to scrub toilets

when we're alone, the Mall speaks to me
over the clucking of the cart and that one wheel
just ceaselessly just spinning in place

the Mall can't seem to understand storefronts
the arcane fire beetle dance of retail
these flimsy aluminum gates
like the retractable teeth of low self-esteem

the Mall wants quiet
it likes to listen to the sound of its own crumbling
it shudders at the simultaneous conversations of consumers
how their volume pig-piles like violence

the Mall yearns, more than anything
to sink into the earth
so it can one day be discovered again
and mistakenly called holy

you can tell things that were crafted by human beings
because they need to be cleaned

I bleed minutes into the punch clock
and it feeds my pockets this lopsided geometry

I am a shit-sucker
an age-scrubber

I will scrape up all of the food that you purchase
but deem unworthy of your mouth
I will wipe away all of the things too dirty
for the body to hold
all the dirt revealed by morning
scrubbing the hollow lungs
of the lonely leviathan of commerce

the strength of the mountains
is the soft despair of scenery
the silent melancholy of furniture

Me & the Mall, we are the lavender
we are the darkness of the infinite infinite

drill a hole in me that I might be a star
that I might be somewhere
instead of this marching

this is why workers work
because we do not know
which movement we make will
lead us to our salvation

I am a broken wheel
and I refuse to stop spinning

HOMELESS

Ahead of me on the sidewalk
a paper cup is asking for spare change and I do
what every asshole in front and behind me does
I look at my feet, look at the cars, the sky,
as if poverty were a disease you could catch by paying attention,

But at that last moment I make the fatal mistake
and I look that paper cup in the eyes
and it says
"Hey man, I hope I didn't wake you when I left the house this morning."
and I place the face,
Last night, this crumpled pair of eyes and cardboard flag
had come in with my roommate, Luke

May:
Luke and I had been together since September
Scratch-ticket roommates coupled by the landlord,
With child-eyed shame he told me his junkie back-story
and I fell for the romance of our kitchen-sink gothic

Dirty-blonde dirty loophole Luke, of sun-sweat worries and sour mouth
EBT cards and disability checks were in the mailbox
until the drinking, Luke, you were not able to maintain

June:
Addiction isn't an injury, it isn't a wound.
It's closer to madness…
an extra skull wrapped around your head,
another body slathered on top of your skin

When you went missing from the methadone clinic
your refrigerator hummed the empty days pacing
in the thirty-rack afternoon

You turned your lazy insect hands to the pockets
of other chemical dependents to survive

So there was Barry,
who looked like a bruised and dented low-rent porn-star
He was good for extra painkillers
and cleaned the kitchen in the morning

Little Mike, pushing seventy, he paid rent for a while
but it was impossible to look him in his
boiling and moth-eaten face

The hard-drinking anti-depressant teenagers
who wandered in and out like lost Atlantans

There was Tracy, Luke's part-time fire engine

And then there was Me, the shivering sorry-handed janitor

July:
Death can take you and you can yet live
It's actually a very common thing

Luke, your humanity seeped out of you
into unsightly couch-stains
A home disappearing into your dried-up
crack burnt blood, reeking of a recycling center

Our apartment not much more
than a vacant lot tug-of-war

You're in the alley trying to kick the back door down
bang bang bang - Brian, let me in - bang bang bang

August:
Saw you buried.

Your liver finally buckling under the slow snake hammer of hepatitis
and now, I can't look homeless men in the face
because I'm terrified that they'll be You,
like there was one last loophole

As impossible as the rest of your life,
every paper cup is your outstretched hand
just out of reach

So yeah, you can have my money
but no,
I don't have anything to spare

REALITY TELEVISION

A handful of miles outside of the city
Reality Television gets out of bed, sleepless
just after dawn and drives three miles
to the Cuban convenience store that
still sells Lucky Strike filters

He buys a multi-pack of hardcore magazines
throws away two of them
He likes the ones with surprising or vague titles
like Mug Sluts or Chisel Azz

Unless the models are missing a few teeth,
or are helplessly scarred, or have a rash
on their genitals, he can't come
but no one knows how their lust was made

He masturbates in his car, in the parking lot
hoping to be caught
his dry rough hands often wearing blisters into his cock

He spends the rest of the morning
at the airport, drinking sweet expensive drinks
awash in the malcontent denizens of nowhere
Reality Television is a people watcher
it gets him in trouble, he forgets he can be seen
he forgets he has a body

on nights when he's skipped work he's come to near-
blows with men he didn't realize
he was staring at
mistaken for a sexual predator
which he thinks he is so similar to
but Reality Television could never muster
the arrogance

drunk in the afternoon, he wants to know
how long it takes other people
to become not him
staring into strangers and wondering
how deep or shallow he is inside of them
how much time they take, in the morning,

in the dark, or maybe with the lights on
zipping up and gluing down their
other person costumes

Depending on the day of the week
or the time of the year, Reality Television
has to be at the studio as late as four
but sometimes as early as noon

Getting home in the warlock hours
he lays in bed, restless, thinking about the ancient gods
if they ever leaned so close to their looking pools
that they fell into the eyes of Odysseus
if the immortals, looking down, ever yearned
to be trapped in the labyrinth

BEEKEEPER

When I was six years old
I invented a machine that re-arranged
the timeline of my life
So that instead of happening chronologically,
the moments of my life happened in order of importance
Now my life began the first time I saw a piano
and will end the 2nd time I punch Keith Bowes

When I was nine years old
Parken Reidell and I chased a peacock
into the woods to catch it,
Parken stepped in a hornet's nest and ran
I stood still, believing that if I didn't move
the hornets would not harm me

I received thousands of stings,
the hornets filling my mouth, scraping across my eyes,
climbing into my ears,
they've never left

My brain is a beekeeper.

After nine years old, I stopped sleeping,
waking again and again in the night,
the bees trying to cut their way out

I didn't get a full night's sleep until I was sixteen,
when I learned to masturbate
Now I fuck like a monster
because sex is the opposite of nightmares

Ugly girl, you keep looking to me for answers
but you know my brain is just a nest of bees,
so don't be surprised that all that comes out of my mouth
is stinging

You moved your hands towards my body and I stood still
believing that no one would be hurt
I kept my back rigid,
my fists clenched tight

but it just made it easier for the nightmares
to get in through my ears

Speak up, I can't hear you
over this buzzing choir of shame

When I was seven years old the worst part about
pissing myself in class
was NOT when my first grade teacher
came over and shook her head at me
like I was the ugliest dog in the world,
but it was the minutes before she found out about the mess;
trapped in that steamy puddle,
the hot urine scraping between my skin and my corduroys

Ugly girl, every time I remember that you've seen me naked
my scalp feels like that. piss rash in first grade,
piss rash in first grade,
like hornets chewing on the roots of my hair
of my hair

Unlike Parken, who got two stings and ran
I stood still,
a frightened and paralyzed child

It takes ugly to know ugly,
So ugly girl, I'm gonna call you what we are
what we are

Every time you use the word beautiful I wish
I could invent a machine
at the end of my life

When I was six years old I invented a machine
that ensured that I would be born
the day after the day I died
On that day,
my grandmother looked at my thin,
strong hands and told me
I should become a piano player
I should've listened to her

Maybe then I would
have better known how
to use my hands

THE MAYOR OF THE 21ST CENTURY

Alistair Zob, King of the Living Pinballs,
maybe-just-maybe could have made it
to the front of the line to the bathroom
but not me, motherfucker,
even though it was my own fucking house,
so I peed out my bedroom window

John Duce's 25th brought turnstile party pegs,
polished with their beautiful ammunition,
through the multiplying doors of the third floor
and unevenly cluttered the living spaces that
complained to me in their usual body language

My wooden floors hate this.
My living room likes warmth and family,
not the cold precision of twentysomethings
flirting in the half-dark

My kitchen likes to get things accomplished
Instead, it's been turned into
the World' Least Interesting Graveyard,
a tangle of miserable inky peacocks
with shoulders bursting with piercings and arrogance

You can stand around and NOT talk to me anywhere!
Why did you come to my house to do it?

I go out to the porch
to get a refreshing breath of cigarette
and fall into a conversation about sculpture
with a pair of sunglasses
And the sunglasses say to me,
"I've got a gorgeous ass."
And I say to them, "I know you've got a gorgeous ass,
but I'm not going to admit that to you,
because I'm jealous of attractive people,
so can we please just talk about
what we're actually talking about?"

She says to me, "Look at my midriff"
And I say to her,
"Listen Lady, I don't have a pantheon of gods in my refrigerator,
I don't have the epic lifestyle you're looking for.
I'm not special, I'm not interesting;
The Heart of Saturday Night is not playing on the stereo,
the essence of summertime isn't seeping out of the bed-sheets,
and the Mayor of the Twenty-First Century doesn't live here!"

And the sunglasses say to me,
"So... what do you... do?"
And she's not asking me how I get from
one side of each moment to the other
She's not asking me how I cope
with the responsibility of perspective
She's asking what quirky ornaments I've gathered
for my personality
And I admit to her that I
write poetry

And she says to me,
"Yeah... I don't like poetry all that much...
I don't think it's very... good."
And I should ask her what it is about the oral tradition
she doesn't like
Why she doesn't think that art's first venue
is all that great

What's wrong with the open place where the world
and the earth come to rest upon one another
Why she doesn't enjoy it when fact and myth
simultaneously conform to the manifold
of unconcealed being

Instead I look that pair of sunglasses in the eyes
and tell them,
"So, I mean this with as little offense as possible,
but I don't think you know what the fuck
you're talking about."

THIS REFUSES TO BE A SECRET (MARS)

I was trying to catch my breath
I lost it hunting for Mars
I lost it on the rocks
near the sand
in the curve of the sea spray
I lost it kissing seashells
and wishing tall ships to crash upon me
Mars is not in the ocean

I was running across the sky
My forehead digging into the asphalt
My shoulders digging a trench down the Jamaicaway
slicing a line to you
I was the reason for all that construction on the BU Bridge

I was trying to grow planets in your living room
I nurtured them with sunsets
At night trying to sing them to sleep with time
Time being a song a borrowed from your lips

Mars is not the moon of war
10,000 miles beneath its surface
a battery of vermilion philosophers
is trying to discover where we already are
So excuse my futon mumbles
Excuse my sunrise

Mars is making me yumyum sleepy coocoo
I am caught in the slow folds of your body
Your lazy heavy curves
The sustained melt/melt, melt/melt
The sweet glue fables in your eyes

Are these your elbows?
Or are they tourniquets?
If I asked you nicely, would you tighten them around
my cowardice until I made love to you?

COUCH-SICK

Just inside the front door there was a small
room to your left rented by Smudge and his girlfriend
Tony and Swiss shared one of the two proper
bedrooms, where they built themselves
bunk beds out of scrap wood we found
in the street including three police barricades
a weight-bench, a little girls' dresser and a player piano

It never stopped them from having sex
at all hours of the night
and I should know because they'd
wake me up to tell me
"hey, hey, Peter hey"
"what?"
"I think I just took Leslie's ass pass"

But this was Allston in the early aughties
so even the dudes living the bunk-bed lifestyle
were still partying like all calendars
had just disavowed any knowledge of permanence

My bedroom was the six feet between
the turn in the wrap-around couch and the wall
plus all the milk crates I could jam under that back table

I slept with my head under the only
window in the room, a ground-level arrow slit
that constantly dribbled sound like the slack
moan of the dozing guilty

The only one who didn't share a room was Queen
my freshman high school best friend
who reinvented our hometown in that brittle
subterranean shanty just barely buried
under the brick-scabbed world

There was a strict house party schedule
the early evenings crackled
like the outer ring of the vinyl before-slip of the fader
and: warm bodies

The traffic lights of cell phones' wet chirping studded the air
drowsy with flirting
voices tangling around voices
a carousel of yarn catching
the city in our momentum

My five a.m. grocery store job stared at me
from out of the Michelob-stained oven clock
but I couldn't sleep even if the sound would let me
my body nauseous from couch
the hours of the weekend worn skintight like month-
long unwashed clothes rediscovered in new
combinations each morning like finding different
dance partners in the same circle of friends

We're all crammed in the single-file hallway of the night
backs against the door-frames
sliding past one another
You're going to get another drink
I ought to be leaving

Queen always left the kitchen before
it stopped pounding with dancefloor-
fed bass with casket speakers
and rumbling the molten curses of the old gods
he's trapped in his room, hollowing out
his flesh from the inside
with alabaster chemical More

When all of the motion has carved its way
out of the face of the tile
Me & Rosie would stay awake through Boston's
aquamarine gloaming, me on the couch, her
on the floor, babbling on into workweek kind of hours
letting me leer at the top 3/4th of her breasts

I am terrified to speak of the trajectory of my life
I am terrified of all that is coming out of my eyes
I am terrified of my brain: it is a record player
built by a man that I've never met

I am terrified of the speed of my best friend's heart
he's alone in his room
carving his mother's disease
into the tollbooth of addiction

We are orphans
raised by ghosts
betrayed by the twentieth century
growing ever-smaller in the distance

LIVING ROOMS

We are the living room and we watch them
They live outside us and underneath us
we live in the sky its name is Ceiling
they are not like us, they move, they move
like dead light in the fog, like river in the dark
like mountains when no one is looking

they move their hands toward us and we grow
a battery of discarded miscellany
drop-ceiling garden of retired appliance
we are equipment untethered from context
like language unlearned

My name is Maskingcymbaltwine
there are many of them that live under the sky of us
but mostly there are five

they have a game called Ball-Ball
they play in the living room, things get broken
when they play, it is where we come from
I think the ball is their father

My name is Fishinglineturntable
my favorite is the one we named Cassette Player
his voice boom-box bounces across the earth
whose name is The Floor
he plays ball the least

I have met the ball he has put his smash to me
the name of the ball is The Devil
when things on earth die they wake up and are one of us
before you wake up your name is Asleep

My name is Galvinizedspiderwebmarimbanailhalo
my favorite is the one we named County Fair
He is out. Everything about him is out.
from his ferris wheel legs to his snow-covered eyes he is shedding

I think he dreamed me. I know in my heart
that I am a long dream. I do not think things get broken
because of the ball, but because they are not dreamed enough

My name is Acousticrollingpin and I remember
I remember before I was hung on this ceiling
I remember when I was two different things
a rolling pin and an acoustic guitar
now that I am combined I am more than the sum of my parts
I no longer have strings but I still have song
I no longer bake bread but I can still feed
I am not broken

My favorite is the one we named Dance of Dead Cranes
he is the slowest and the fastest
he is like on-off, on-off
he is like an amplifier that can hear itself

My name is Suitcaseonoff
I know a song and it is called Closed
the lyrics are: electricity
I know another song and it is called Open
the lyrics are: silence
the ones that made me are not one or the other
they are like the act of breaking
they move, and when they move
they move faster than choices

My favorite is the one we named Skyscraper
his shoulders are a knife, his hair is a knife, his chin is a knife
his smile is a knife, his laugh is a knife

My name is Yellow Stool, I am broken
but I am intact
I am hung on the wall sideways by an electrical cord
strung up at the same time as these
other misplaced objects, these trophies
to nothing in particular

I do not understand, I am a stool
when I am placed on the floor
you can sit or stand upon me
I have no purpose on the ceiling

Their friends come over and say
we are very interesting
that we are exciting "decoration"
Sometimes, I think that I am not a stool at all

My favorite is the one we named Haunted House
he appears to be lost, the name
of his bedroom is Couch, he talks to us
when he is alone

My name is Milkcratechandelier

My name is Fiberglasswindowfender

My name is Confettistryrofoamdiscowreckingball

My name is the White Horse and I speak
my language is the electric human
I was made to be a part of a child's swing-set
it was broken and I was thrown away
I was found by these humans and hung
in their living room
where every available surface is smothered spare parts
but we are not extraneous we are necessity

I speak the secrets of mirrors and headlights and light-sockets
where my language lands the environment
alters to everything other than usual
my language is freedom in every direction

I have shed the anguish of mannequins
I have survived beyond purpose
I am the outside-in
I still contain the world of the hands that made me
I am the origin of author and story
I am a photograph of a billion species of flesh

FALLING OFF MY BICYCLE

The BEST PART of falling off of your bicycle
is not when your skin peels
like the petals of an artichoke,
cuticles melting into milk,
or when your elbow
spits the fingertips of your heart
deep into the sweaty tarmac.

It's when you get up.
It's when you stand up off the street so fast
that you threaten to take it with you.

When you tornado your bicycle to your breast as if
it were the one who was bleeding.

This is the same kind of everyday miracle as
a lover unraveling their jeans for you,
the kind of hummingbird moment
like when you remember the power of your heels
to rebuke the quicksand of icicles.

ELEGY FOR THE CASSETTE TAPE

When I was six years old
there was only one way I could get to sleep:
A centimeter-wide magnetic strip
that contained Dr. Seuss's "If I Ran the Zoo."
Later that same year I saw *Back to the Future*
for the first time
and the next day I fought with my older brother
until he caved in and bought me
Chuck Berry's Greatest Hits

I listened to that tape until it broke
When it did I became a combat surgeon,
opening it up and using my mother's sewing scissors
to cut the scotch tape to the perfect width,
because my salvation lived in that plastic ribbon
The cassette tape is physical

It's the difference between getting porn off the internet
and going to a XXX movie theatre:
Masturbation should be dangerous.

Your tapes lived along with you
I had a small beige briefcase
with latches on each end, and I absconded
with my siblings' cassettes until it was filled
The final tape was the holy grail…
The Green Plaid Album by The Mighty Mighty Boss-Tones

And that clunky black tape player, which was heavier
than anything I owned until I was eleven,
which was rescued from the attic or the basement
and you had to press down on the play button real smooth-like
or the whole thing got jammed, but
I could do it just right
because me and that machine, we knew each other

Had spent many nights together
in the back of the Lincoln, volume turned to one so as not
to wake my mother in the passenger seat
Feeling the whirr of the spools travel into my shoulder,
mouthing the words to "Norwegian Wood"
which I could barely hear over the crackle

I liked the Beatles
They made albums you could listen to
beginning to end,
because jumping around from song to song
is a pain in the ass on a cassette

This September a friend of mine gave me his old walkman
and when I rode the T the people around me
were plugged into these digital boxes with
eighteen-gazatrillion songs
that are never enough
Meanwhile, in my bag, I had *Desire* and *Pearl*
and they were the only two albums I needed

So you can listen to music that
will go with you anywhere
but I wanna listen to music so necessary
I'll do anything to get to it,

Gorge yourself on this thin creativity all you want
I'd rather consume art with presence
Maybe a little hiss and crackle

The cassette tape was trying
to teach us something about economy
The cassette tape didn't become obsolete,
we just got boring
It's not that the future is coming faster and faster
It's that the past wants nothing to do with us

54

BALL

Ball is a full-body, cardiovascular sport
that requires the use of (1) one oversized tennis ball
and (2) as many players as you can find

The ball is passed from player to player
as quickly as humanly possible
and, when deemed necessary
adding impossibly fluid dance like moves
to the act of passing
(See also: the reverse-top, the cabaret,
and the blind switchblade)

For increased fun, try smashing
your friends' faces with the ball

You can really get your point across
using your own head or face to hit them

Advanced players will throw a fake-out into the mix
(See also: the sideways bottle opener, the delayed
street fighter, and the Thoughtful Flamingo)

The sport is best played indoors, allowing
for hilarious ricochet eventualities

Hopefully, you have downstairs neighbors
and Ball creates an opportunity
for you to meet and become friends with them

Complete detachment from the ownership
of material possessions is required
to play Ball

Things will get spilled and smashed
When they do, view these things as
only being changed
See them as improved

Remember, Window, whether you
are smooth or splintered you are still splitting light

Like all deconstructionist sports, Ball
has no winner or loser
The happening of the game happens
in the presence of happening rising
up into the moment where the players
realize the game has occurred
when moving into the past and the future
pales in comparison to the importance of Ball

Your cities are filled with uncommon children
living behind every single door

Each morning this broken furniture
wakes up to carve strange new hobbies & sacrament
out of their scattershot histories

With every head-butt, every hip-buck
we are cracking the invisible rituals
of someone's else culture

We are swinging, kicking and sweating
We are spinning around each other, spinning
the dream of our lives around
the sightless earth

There's this old trick:
to forget that you're alive to summon
the rush of remembering that you are
but I want you to know
You don't have to

SATURN'S PROMISES

Our palms were aching to grasp those handlebars
so we did, Saturday night, riding three bicycles
deep in the margin of a city that cares more
about tunnels than kindness

Monday will tell you that Saturday
is a slut and a liar but Thursday understands
the fiction of weekends
so we gave ourselves over to pyrotechnic fables
of Saturn's promises the way we gave
our knees over to the manic grammar
of those whirling gears
hyacinths blooming across our kite-tail skin

The two-lane world shimmered like it had opinions
sliding down Boston's french horn streets
the balls of our feet lapping the ricochet
of the streetlight amber snore, we were
bang crash free like gossip
burning apricot cannonball fast, as wide as the heat

We had places to go

Joe lost the address of the party
and J*me wasn't picking up his phone
so we trailed the most interesting pedestrians
we could find and rediscovered our destination

We sweat-whispered slipped-up carbon-
copy staircase to rickety triple-decker house party
where we occupied our hands with bad decisions
and loitered in the kitchen
sandpapering our skin attractive
or at least take-homeable

Searching the atlas of a stranger's face for the billboard
that reads:
Yes, Absolutely, You exist, Stop Worrying
Your actions are more than stumbling in wet sand
quickly swallowed like sunset in the stomachs
of whales which is why their secrets
sound like Valkyries

Looking to remember or forget at the bottom
of an anonymous red cup
and by the time you come out again
you're trapped behind a locked door
handcuffed to the sink
because nowhere in the world is more
exciting than someone you've never met's bathroom
forehead leaning into the medicine
chanting a breakup poem to baseball
and you say:

I am an immigrant from a land called Pine Trees
I've come here, like every one else
to wrestle with the saint of tentacles

My gender is not the most important thing about me
not nearly as important as how I feel about bicycles
so listen, the next time I'm riding and you think
that I'm in the way of your car

Don't Honk

Just Hit Me

And when the blood in my cheeks Rorschachs
against the windshield, don't step on the brakes
let's see how far we can go together
when all of my orchards are crushed under
your scaffolding of personal wealth
the spectre of my legs will leap up
and steal all of your movie memories

Are you ready to share my oxygen with me?
Are you ready to let go of this sink
unlock that door
step into the easy light
and become important

BLIND AS PUMP-PUMP

mistakes are falling off me like loose hair,
mistakes are forming lists in my mind,
and mistakes are being added to lists
to lists as quickly as pump-pump,
pump-pump and I have to get to you
I am on the train and it is moving too slowly,
the world is in my way
everything around me is moving as slowly
as my first grade teacher saying the word "underachiever"
And wait… why the fuck am I at Kendall?
I went too far on the Red Line,
I am as blind as pump-pump, pump-pump
I am shoving out of the train, running across
the diamond-dappled headlight night, into the subway again
and I went into the wrong entrance to Kendall
and mistakes and mistakes
and it's just me and this iron medieval turnstile gate
and I will not lose you
so I am jamming my body through the turnstile
forcing it in a direction it doesn't want to go
and I will forget our anniversary
I will forget the day of your father's death
but I will do this:
smash my face against the sternum of physics
until we are both bloody
my crumbling flesh is painting
crimson streamers across my skin
bruises are blossoming like hungry puddles
on the surface of my skull
and I will not be defeated by my bones

SHHH

it was supposed to be the summer of love
but it was just summer
the heavy air clinging to our windowpanes
gurgling in the continual high noon

your bed is a lollipop in an oven
we never say i love you
so I'll use the word ... kumquat

I admit, I came after you like a collapsing elevator
you were in the basement
keeping your ribs warm with photo albums

I admit, I knew how to find you because
we both left ourselves for alone
you pretended not to know how to dance until you held me

60

I hid the summer in the heels of my wrists
until the day they exploded unfettered
across the central square skyline

the heat will come and go as it pleases

all of the betrayal that I have set sail
upon the sea has soon come back to me
my mirror has survived fists heavier than yours
you can scream in my cheekbones if you want to
you don't have to kumquat quietly

we both have been hiding in our own clenched prayers
unbuckle your knuckles and tear open your whispers
there's an infra-red Vesuvius erupting out of the valley of your chest
your spine rolled sidewise across my lap
like the industrial revolution in reverse
I feel more organic each moment

your shoulder blades are stumbling tulips
under silk, shaking off dreams
of milk and birthday mystery
the summit of your hipbone was a red desk I once owned

the triangle of springtime
that hovers above the folds between your legs
is what dawn would look like
if glaciers could fly
you're not the first person to think
that you were never going to kumquat again

don't forget your flesh at the pillow

STEPHEN RADIO

Stephen Radio has heroes
but still doesn't know how to spend his time

He finds himself most weekends in strangers' kitchens
in apartments that want to be starships,
and, if he's lucky,
the window's open and the leopards spill out
onto the shoulders of Boston, beloved city
Eldritch swamp colossus

Stephen Radio likes rooftops
He hunts for parties for the chance to scale the crowns of buildings,
making friends with Allston High Plains BBQers
and Mission Hill art school cat burglars

He pushes his way past bathroom hallways filled with boys
with wrists and elbows like scissors and board games
and girls with eyes lurking under bangs like deadly swingsets

Maybe you know him,
maybe you can tell from his name:
Stephen Radio has his eyes fixed on the sky
He only knows where his feet are during wishes

He's a simple boy, he's no greaseball tightpants
with steam engine thighs
There are earnest dreams sprinkled on his cheekbones

He's trapped in the upper margin of the hub of the universe
where fire insinuates itself into the rust of the clouds
and the dotted lines of constellations come into focus

And the rooftop argument is always the same,
and the glowing coral mercury windows say
"You will not find what you are looking for up there"
And Stephen Radio says
"I will not stop looking

I can taste these rooftops through my sneakers
I can taste the sky through my sneakers
The frozen descending marine songs of clouds
are attached to my shoulders
The stars live between my eyelashes"

And the shattered desert choir of bricks say
"You
Will not find what you are looking for up there

You are lost

You are lost like the insomniac kite flyers
who cannot rise above the living nightmare of a dead family
and settle for windtangled orphancy
You are lost like cars, and lamps, and candles
You are lost like the moon has lost the sun
for the sake of the earth"

Stephen Radio says
"The trees know why we run
We turned one blonde unblinking eye to the ocean
and went wolf on oxygen
Our jeans can turn these streets into forests
Our fingers can turn rooftops to magic
Boston is a god
I will not stop looking"

And all of the lost baseballs ask

"How can there be a god in heaven
if there are so many here on earth?"

Stephen Radio says
"The whole of the concealed divinities
of the sky can balance upon open eyelids
Understand that to preserve is an active adventure of the heart"

And the ghosts of weathervanes howl
"The more you look, the less you'll see
It is impossible to learn
how to not touch something by touching it

The harder you search for the openness
of the world the more you will find
the concealment of the earth

The mystery is always the mystery
and it is never anything else

You
Will not find
what you are looking for up there"

Stephen Radio says
"I will not stop looking
There are questions that curl like saltwater
There are questions that smother like marbles
There are questions that smother like a front-end crash
and a ten-ankle pile-up

But there are answers that can hold you like skin
There are answers that breathe back
There are answers that can spread like radio signals

I will not stop looking for them."

OPEN LETTER TO BOYS WHO THINK THAT THEY'RE BIGGER THAN ME

Somewhere in my past
there is a small boy
walking across a two-day field
of un-touched snow
frozen overnight

He is trying not to break the surface
leaving the canvas of winter unspoken
To accomplish this
he is holding his breath
as if that will make him lighter
as if that will pull him into the air

Welcome to the Age of my body
Welcome to the Age of my body, Animal
That's a nice square head you've got there, Kid
good for miniature examples of physics
Something the ancient Greeks would enjoy
like nailing shit

Welcome to the rattlepedal of my voice, Delta male
Your biceps keep sizing me up
Your tits are staring at me
The smooched pennies of your nipples are licking
the nervous giraffe of my ribcage with photons
Your skin is filled, head to toe, with arm floaties
but they will not keep you safe
and they will not let you levitate

I am not this thin because I am friends with sorrow
but she did teach me to whittle down my mirror
like I was the last heir to New Hampshire

So you think you're a Real Big Noise, don't ya, Racecar?
Well, I've got this 72pt sign language popping outta my hip-bones
screaming, *I love you back*
into the slide trombone of your violence

If you think that my T-cells have something to teach you,
then I will invite my blood into the tumble wash of your knuckles
until your hands are soaked with learning
I'm real good at getting beat up
and the confetti of my nose has been scribbling
welcome... welcome... welcome...
for about eighteen years now

Welcome to the Age of Meat, Fleshsack

Sorrow wanted me to tell you:
sleep is nothing like death
sleep is a function of the body
and the playground of dreams
where my body was woven together
from the spirits of rope ladders
and hammered into the shape of a cigarette
So like all good prayers, I burn

66

I have become exactly like the man I imagined my father was
while he was away, not raising me

Our fathers were probably hiding in the same city, Big Man
while we became descendants of our own dreams

I am not a child of god
but I know how to walk across the surface of snow
without leaving any tracks

I cannot teach you how to do this
but I'll tell you a secret:
It's got nothing to do with weight

PUSH, PUSH, PUSHING

Oh, Oh, Oh, Hello, Hello
My name is Flapjack
I am a dog
I have four legs
I am glad to meet you, you
smooth paw'd tail-empty person
I am glad to meet you, you
Hair-deprived symphony of scent
I am a dog
and I have four legs
and I do four things:
1. Eat
2. Rest
3. Run
4. Hold together heaven and sky and earth
and mortals and the impossible
with the strength of my responsibility
And I know what you're thinking, I know
number three and four are redundant
but running gets its own number
because running is important

I've got all this push, push, pushing inside of my legs
and when I run, the earth turns

And I know what you're thinking, I know
I didn't include having fun on the list
but fun is part of my responsibility
Fun keeps the body powerful
and the mind sharp

You should see the amazing feats I am capable of!
Watch how delicately I place
your tokens of appreciation
in the chainsaw of my mouth
And these are not just twigs and rocks
these are tree trunks and mountains that I lift
so softly between my razor's-fist of teeth

And sometimes I get so excited
about these feelings that I feel
that I just have to press my face against the air
like this:

>photograph of tree<

There
is this hollow thing inside of my body
and I try to keep my mouth open
as much as I can, to try to fill it with wind

But there is only the mumbling that comes
from the basement of all open fields
where my heart was sown together
with threads of azure grass

And I know,
I know that they say that the moon is a lady,
but
I have heard the voice of the King of Shapeshifters
and one day he will say my name

and I will loose a call from my tongue
like a jackknife hoard of bats
lifting beyond the silver nothing

And I will surrender
the devouring

NEW HAMPSHIRE

I'm sweeping the floor
in apartments in my twenties
and I look a little too closely for a little too long
into the wooden floor

I pack up my things and sweep,
closing the door behind me,
looking for new bedrooms, like seventh grade,

Southern New Hampshire,
those dark green fields, and brown hills
rolling around bends of nothing

we were as poor as the Merrimac

I remember missing seventh grade
when everyone else became a teenager
while I slept
I got out of bed and stayed a child for another nine years
and women still look at me like I'm Christopher Robin

I remember picking out houses, checking buildings
for any homes to be had
I remember searching the wood,
the vintage framework for something
I could fall in love with
with carpet from the nineteen- seventies
that reminded me of photographs of my uncles
when they were beautiful and impossible

sometimes I look at you like you're an empty building
I'm wandering around in like when I was in seventh grade

looking for a someplace I could find a bedroom in,
while my parents are outside,
are wondering where all the money went

and I'm not sorry
because sometimes you look at me
like you're a photograph from my family's past
when my father's cousins owned bright red cars

and bright white suits with collars as wide as forever
sometimes you look at me like you are
six-and-1/2 inches beyond the rope swing
as you sail past the zenith of its trajectory
in a Southern New Hampshire summer
that's as unstoppable as a black and yellow speedboat

and it's unfair,
it's as unfair as the Merrimac,
as unfair as seventh grade
as children

your ethereal fingerprints
your tapping foot
the way you smoke cigarettes like the rain has coffee in it
the way you softly twist the corners of your mouth
like you've got some exquisite understanding
of the human condition

70

the way the sheets of ice on the insides of your irises
crack and melt
in the heat of my bloody and flushed cheeks
like the way the sheets of ice
cracked and melted in the spring
when I was in eighth grade
and lived in New Hampshire

SELF-PORTRAIT

I wake up and I'm already driving and it's 9 p.m. in
the morning on one of those nights where I've been up
for three days the back of my tongue smells like burnt
fiberglass and I swallow a couple more 'diet' pills

on 93 the last lonely lights of sleeping gas stations
refract and blur across my greasy windshield and cut long
vertical lines strobing across my vision this is way too familiar

I wake up

I'm back in the convenience store behind the counter
counting the cigarettes which are really my choir
of one-thousand-faced madmen I imagine cigarettes
have southern accents cartons of cigarettes are fifty dollars
and when they're delivered they come in boxes of twenty

we get about ten boxes each week I'm just saying
you'd make alot of money robbing a cigarette delivery guy

I wake up

and I realize I've just walked two blocks with my
eyes closed I'm a little lost now caught in
the webs of streets Cape Cod hides because god
forbid, a tourist realizes poor people live here

I wake up

and the darkness on the other side of the bed is pissed
at me we were having a conversation about how I never
do anything but sleep anymore and I fell asleep
paranoia holds my eyes open in case she starts talking
again I wait a long time

I wake up

and I'm swing dancing with the middle lane of 495
barreling south for a reason I can't recall and in my
sleep- deprived dementia it doesn't occur to me to pull
over and take a nap and I don't know if my body can
unravel enough miles to get me home

in this moment
I want that the moments of my life were bunched
together like the branches of a snowflake so I
could spin about my life in sweeping spirals like the
way the streets of Hyannis spider-web
away from the airport rotary

I wake up

and I am washing windows in my janitor's uniform
dirty with the stains of bleach and ammonia
that reek of the opposite of life

I wake up

and I'm in the cab and the dispatcher is screaming

**95! this is why we don't hire twenty-motherfucking-
year-old cab drivers! are you there? 95!**

I wake up

and my junkie roommate, Luke, is standing over me
holding the telephone out like a bomb
the tiny voice of the manager
of Kaybee Toys telling me I'm late for work

I wake up

and I'm laying on the floor of my room next to my bed
which is empty and in a pool of my own vomit
my head hurts so much you can hear my teeth vibrating
my stomach so empty the vacuum of it yanks on my
tonsils every time I dry heave my bones are cold and
my legs are chattering I want to be in any other location
of my life except this sweating shaking crying this is the
kind of pain that tastes like all of the aluminum monsters
of the world screaming at once

I try to climb on my bed and fail, mind you, my bed is
just two mattresses stacked on top of one another
flat on the floor
so like the shoplifter that I am
I ask the god I don't believe in for help
make him promises, try to cut a deal

dear god: if you move me to another place in my life
tomorrow I'll start doing all the things I keep
telling other people they ought to
tomorrow I'll wake up and go to one of those
protests I keep getting emails about
tomorrow I'll wake up and go do something nice
for my mother
tomorrow I'll wake up and go do something nice for
the homeless guy I've been snubbing for two days now
tomorrow I'll wake up and give a gift to everyone
who's never attempted suicide
a little box filled with the opposite of band aids
little plastic strips that heal you before you get hurt

tomorrow I'll wake up tomorrow I'll wake up

I wake up

and my eyes are already open

UNCONTROLLED EXPERIMENTS IN FREEDOM

ABOUT THE AUTHOR

BRIAN S. ELLIS began performing his poetry for audiences in the spring of two thousand six. Since then he has been on the Cantab Lounge Poetry Slam team twice and has represented the Cantab at the individual world poetry slam. He is a local slam champion and has been featured at poetry venues from New England to various regions of the U.S. His fast paced, colorful voice is a strong addition to the Boston spoken word tradition.

OTHER GREAT WRITE BLOODY BOOKS

THE LAST AMERICAN VALENTINE: ILLUSTRATED POEMS TO SEDUCE AND DESTROY
24 authors, 12 illustrators team up for a collection of non-sappy love poetry
Edited by Derrick Brown

WHAT IT IS: WHAT IT IS
Graphic Art Prose Concept book
by Maust of Cold War Kids and author Paul G. Maziar

LIVE FOR A LIVING
New Poetry compilation
by Buddy Wakefield

SOME THEY CAN'T CONTAIN
Classic Poetry compilation
by Buddy Wakefield

SCANDALABRA
(Winter 2008)
New poetry compilation
by Derrick Brown

I LOVE YOU IS BACK
Poetry compilation (2004-2006)
by Derrick Brown

BORN IN THE YEAR OF THE BUTTERFLY KNIFE
Poetry anthology, 1994-2004
by Derrick Brown

LETTING MYSELF GO
Bizarre God Comedy & Wild Prose
by Buzzy Enniss

COCK FIGHTERS, BULL RIDERS, AND OTHER SONS OF BITCHES
(Winter 2008)
An experimental photographic odyssey
by M. Wignall

THE CONSTANT VELOCITY OF TRAINS
New Poetry
by Lea Deschenes

CITY OF INSOMNIA
New Poetry
by Victor Infante

HEAVY LEAD BIRDSONG
New Poems
by Ryler Dustin

STORIES LEADING UP TO, AND SOME INCLUDING, E. LEON SPAUGHY
New Short Fiction Pieces
by Matty Byloos

NO MORE POEMS ABOUT THE MOON
by Michael Roberts

THE WRONG MAN
(Winter 2009)
Graphic Novel
by Brandon Lyon & Derrick Brown

SOLOMON SPARROWS ELECTRIC WHALE REVIVAL
by Buddy Wakefield, Anis Mojgani, Derrick Brown, Dan Leamen & Mike McGee

JUNGLESCENE: UNDERGROUND DANCING IN LOS ANGELES
A sweaty modern photographic historical journey
by Danny Johnson

YOU BELONG EVERYWHERE
(Winter 2009)
A memoir and how-to guide for travelling artists
by Derrick Brown with Joel Chmara, Buddy Wakefield, Marc Smith, Andrea Gibson, Sonya Renee, Anis Mojgani, Taylor Mali & more.

writebloody.com

Breinigsville, PA USA
23 September 2009
224589BV00001B/2/P